SEED ACROSS SNOW

Acknowledgments & Notes

Poems in this collection first appeared in the following magazines (sometimes in slightly different versions):

Arable: "To Dressing Up" and "To Our First Hours Married"; *The Connecticut Review:* "Forgive"; *New Millennium Writings:* "Why I Mother You the Way I Do"; *North American Review:* "Nude Model"; *PMS: PoemMemoirStory:* "Ring" and "Our Neighbor's Flock of Peacocks Wander Over for Another Visit"; *River Styx:* "With a Shiner, My Husband Enters the Flower Shop"; *The South Carolina Review:* "Field Trip to the Neighborhood Firehouse"; *Southern Review:* "To the Outdoor Wedding"; *High Horse!: An Anthology of Contemporary Writing by the Faculty of Spalding University's Brief Residency MFA Program:* "To the Outdoor Wedding" and "Why I Mother You the Way I Do." "Ring" and "Our Neighbor's Flock of Peacocks Wander Over for Another Visit" received 2005 Pushcart Prize nominations. "To the Outdoor Wedding" and "Ring" were republished in *Open24Hours.* "Why I Mother You the Way I Do" was republished in *The Heartland Review.*

I am very grateful to Kate Gale, Mark E. Cull, and the entire staff at Red Hen, particularly Steph Opitz and Sydney Nichols, for their support of my work. I thank the Kentucky Arts Council, the Kentucky Foundation for Women, and Spalding University for grants which supported the writing of many of these poems. The Kentucky Foundation for Women also provided valuable retreat space at Hopscotch House where I was able to collect this manuscript. I wish to express gratitude to my all friends and colleagues at Spalding University's brief-residency Master of Fine Arts in Writing Program. My special thanks go to the poetry faculty: Jeanie Thompson, Molly Peacock, Maureen Morehead, Debra Kang Dean, Greg Pape, and Richard Cecil. Their encouragement and support have helped make this book possible. I could have no better mentor than Sena Jeter Naslund and I am grateful for her continued enthusiasm for my work. I am indebted to Karen J. Mann, Katy Yocom, and Gayle Hanratty for their friendship and professional counsel. And I thank my family, especially Terry. I couldn't have imagined any of this without him.

For Wyatt and Quinn

CONTENTS

PART THREE

SEED ACROSS SNOW

This is what I say to myself while
the night throws a bone on the tablecloth
— Katia Kopovich

OVERTURE

O, come see what has been planted.
How will one woman harvest this night-dark seed?

Once, through the chalky bones of sycamores, the sheriff
          and the man, the father, looked down upon the hull
of an overturned canoe, knocking against the shore.
          In the swollen current, rotting apples washed by,
their families holding fast within their bruised hearts.
          I remember that and I remember, too, how it was
raining the day we sat in the school buses, the silver windows
          and their glassy bubbles and the way we were tossed forward
and we laughed until the sirens commenced. Murmurs rose.
          The children were asking "What's happened?"
"Up there?" "Ahead in the road?" "In front of the school?"
          But we were so young then, it only took a week
or two for the sound of brakes and sirens to draw away
          and in art class we returned to replicating our masked selves
in chalk portraits, faces of children who seemed to have forgotten
          what they had seen in the road. It was as if nothing had happened
until the man who came to install our new carpet . . .
          so familiar, I thought, as I picked up book bags, shoes, and coats—
ah! of course! I'd gone to school with him! We laughed finally
          recognizing that. Did we know anything then? Remember
Mr. Blackburn? Mrs. Klein? I realized I had just thought
          of his brother, having read in the newspaper his name
with the priest's, but I knew enough to tamp that back down.
          Our children as old as the two dead girls and we
as old as the bus driver whose wipers swished and swished,
          but God help him he could not see. Who could? See that?
And I recall other brakes, and tires skidding, and running. I
          remember running through the snow, how it crunched

beneath my feet and how my chest went *huh, huh, huh* . . . how

a body lay beneath the front tire. A young woman
all elbows and hands, danced awkwardly in the road. She screamed

while a red envelope scuttled across the road and I turned to run
back to call 911, and ran toward the bland pink faces

(like cabbage roses) pressed against cold glass.
What did I say? I knelt down deliberately.

Mrs. Hallahan's been hit. Help Mommy. Stay here. Stay!
I yelled, pitching back the small words as I ran off again.

And, then, I saw her shoe in our yard and shoes spin through
air. And apples bob. And canoes knock hard. And red

envelopes flutter like redbirds aflight. She'd come across the road
to fetch her mail! And in her mail, a valentine! And I remember

tucking the blanket around her, and thinking *oh Regina,*
you're already dead, aren't you? though I began to chant

It's okay. It's okay. I opened up the words, cracked them open
and watched their green puffs float up.

Words are like little spirits that way. And I remember
blood splattered like seed across snow,

and how without notice it melted away and washed down
the road. And I remember the pressed faces

of my children stained against the glass. If I must recall
that our home is a church, then I must also remember

that our lawn is its graveyard.

So, the vet called it a tumor
and the old dog was carried home. Blankets came down

from the hall closet to make a nest where our children slept
with him one last night. Grief settled into the bones

of Wyatt and Quinn. And when the dog was carried
back out and put into the car, their bodies became houses

they did not think they could live within. And my great

grandfather was driven from his house and once
        at the railroad bridge, they found his plow-horse tied
to the trestle. And they found my great-grandfather's trousers.
        Then his shirt, folded, his socks pulled into each other.
Shoes faced, and pointed as if in a soldier's closet. Then,
        two days later . . . his body bumping against the Kentucky shore.
The skiff rocked as the men stood to gaff him
        out of the cold water. And once, a detective showed me
a photograph. "You know him?" I recognized my neighbor, but
        took a moment to consider my answer. What would come
if I said yes? If I said no? A girl had crawled across our lawn and up
        our neighbor's gravel drive where all night she bled inside
the gold egg of their vintage Cadillac. And once,
        in a room with periwinkle walls, the heavy matelasse spread
collapsed to the floor, which was maple yellow
        and gleamed. And once, traffic flowed lightly below.
I remember it was Sunday and a sheer white curtain
        blew into the room. I could see the edge of my suitcase
in the closet. And once a bride's veil flew over
        the farmland of blue grass. And once, a bride sat beside a pool,
and a black champagne bottle floated in its current.
        And once, someone said, "Shh . . .
don't you move." And once, my neighbor was resurrected
        from rehab and returned home wearing a stainless steel halo,
but she didn't know I had saved her life, nor
        that I was her neighbor and in a storm, outside our house,
she stood in a dark skirt that blew from side to side
        like a church bell. She looked up toward the luminous
red lantern of my son's window. And I remember
        opening the door and I called *Regina! Are you all right?*
and she didn't answer, but finally, she drifted back home, and I went
        upstairs and slept on the floor of my son's bedroom, where I heard

my daughter wandering, sleepwalking through the halls.
　　　　She moved like a child who knew things, and I knew
I had walked the same way and so I watched her and wondered
　　　　who had told her these things and when, when
had I not been around? When? When I was her age, I lay
　　　　on the flowered davenport at my grandmother's home
and she told me things no child should know, but still I wanted
　　　　to know: women were beaten so that their faces
held the purple blooms of late roses, men drank themselves
　　　　to tears, so that they were not men to the women
who lived with them, aunties drank lye then, and it was all
　　　　about shame, as it always is, but also about living story.
I recall that now and I recall everything for what do we have
　　　　but the past to parent us? It has been told
because this yellow morning, my little daughter shook me
　　　　awake and asked me to write a poem for her. *What shall I call it?*
I asked, raising on my elbows. She put her finger
　　　　on her lips and looked to the ceiling. A moment later
she said, "I think you should call it 'The Rain Comes Wild'."

And then, the rain began to peck and pock.

PART ONE

Yellow Boat

Lifted into dry dock, where the sun
hits the little yellow boat, it seems
so happy, perched above the bay waters.

But how can this be? It hangs poised in the air,
caught ready in the brink, though insistent
in its wrong direction,

all set to crash into palm and pines of shore.
Opposite. It is the opposite
of what it should be, yet there it is,

in the sunlight, sheen in its grommets,
proud and lighted mast—
the undeniable glee of it

caught showing it's not
what we all know
it to be.

To the Outdoor Wedding

All come, forgive, and bless the dogmatic over-ripe bride
who insists she will be married in the garden

of her dead mother, though the guests and wedding party
hiss and shiver as the light rain turns unrepentantly

to pelting ice. All rise, and love the narrow bridesmaids,
numb and under-dressed in lavender slivers of spaghetti strap,

and listen to their teeth chatter as they scurry down
the aisle, drawn to the collective body heat

of the groomsmen and minister shifting from foot
to foot under the wavering trellis of altar. Praise

the wind picking up mightily, and the groom, unsteady
and sallow, who does not beam when she appears

in blown splendor on her father's arm—and the guests
who are wet-faced, their heads bowed down

to keep the sleet from stinging. It is the bride, prayer-
ful and confident in her white faith, we have to thank

when a gust picks up and wraps her long veil three times
around her father's head, shrouding him from the booming

garden tent about to unpluck itself from the soggy ground.
Who else but her to be thankful to when instead of the tent,

her veil snaps free from the father's flailing and lifts high,
then thrashes away over the Kentucky cornfields, just now

brilliant in their new spring greening—the green shine,
the sumptuous periwinkle sky, the brilliant white strata

folding into itself, and dropping its knot—but wait! Again
the wind sends it sailing and the guests, heads up now,

mouths open in collected prayer of *ah* and *ah* as the veil
transforms into a bucking Chinese dragon, taking away

all that is old, folding, dancing off and far. The guests
gather themselves and offer the warm utterance

ooh when from the thawing and newly planted fields
a thousand black starlings lift in alarm.

LEAVING BEAR COUNTRY

You don't see that every day, I say
to them again and again, until
they do believe it all can be seen
every day, until they believe
each early morning drive holds

the kept promise of a mammoth
black bear, loping in front of us
and across the deserted divided
Highway—dropping off into the deep
ravine that runs alongside the road.

Seconds later, she surfaces;
from her snout, a shake moves
through her loose shaggy shoulders,
shimmying all the way down
to her rough broad rump. Off

the crystal drops fly and up
into the air like feral notes of music.
My kids have seen it all, seem impressed
until they turn from the rear window,
read the sign fast approaching. *Leaving*

Bear County. They roll their eyes
at each other—then snuggle down into
their seats to re-enter their interrupted
dreams, those places where the road ahead
will always—no matter what

I've said—have signs alongside
to notify exactly what they will
see and when, whether or not
I wake them from deep sleep.
My children are full of dogged

dreams that tell them it will be
there—all of it—and each
and every day, when-
ever they choose to wake
and see.

KEEPING WORDS

It stopped their bickering cold
in the back seat, when I turned,
fingertips on temples, and screamed,
"My god you've got to *stop*!
You're giving me a splitting
 hairbrush!" We laughed all the way

through Georgia. But a few months later,
during spring cleaning, my husband stood
in the dark mouth of the attic and stared
below in disbelief. *What?* I asked
sharply, *just hand down the damned
bird cage and let's get on with it.*

The bird cage! I bellowed and stamped
at his lack of comprehension, then
gently, he dropped into my hands
the scalloped and pink, two-
storied, iced like a birthday cake,
Barbie dollhouse. Thanks, I huffed. *Sheesh!*

My doctor says it's nothing, that
like a lot of women my age
I do not sleep enough
to find the right words,
that I should accept a birdcage
as a dollhouse, take solace
in the fact I know she's not
a plumber. And I do. And I realize, too,
that the stainless steel halo screwed
to my neighbor's head is not a halo,

nor is it an astronaut's helmet, keeping
her safe for her next airless journey,

nor is she placed here merely to prove
someone's worse off than me.
                              And ketchup
is not blood though it is rich and sweet, and
a key is not a pencil, though they both waggle
in crooked places. And the small green pond
at the front door does not hold fan-tailed koi,

but cheap goldfish who are not in a womb.
And my newly teenaged son was not, cannot,
will not, but is actually magnificent, and
my daughter did have a dollhouse, beat-up
and crayon stained, and dragged to the curb
where it slumped for three days, not like bird

cage, not the sort, anyway, that I'd want
to keep her in. That cage would be painted
purple and have a safe trapeze. And
my body is not a temple, but asylum; though
my home is a church and when I wake
in the morning and look into the face

of my husband, he is my lover, for who
could not be mad about a man
who resignedly handed down a dollhouse
when his wife demanded a birdcage.
When I look at him, I remind
myself to make labels, stick them

in my favorite books, in a jar of precious
saffron threads, on the watercolor
of Matisse's view over Nimes,
a clean and tidy attic, all those
and other gifts he's given to me. The labels
will all read *husband, husband*

OUR NEIGHBOR'S FLOCK OF PEACOCKS WANDER OVER FOR ANOTHER VISIT

There aren't enough brains among them
to make more than an addled chicken,
but O when they strut through our back yard,
stagger their tails into fluttering
Chinese fans, the children stand at our window
and whimper, ache to shepherd them
into a tight circle, gather hands, listen
to the squawk of sermon, old women's voices
rising in shrieking psalms. Children
and dim, beautiful birds, come together in prayer
to the church of the great and uncouth outdoors.

White Bear

And so, after a few years, it was
given to her anyway, though
then certainly
too late for her
to have the child
he would not agree
to. That night
she watched him
go darkly from
their bed to tend
the fire; she did not
see him, but knew
he knelt naked, trembling
before the chilling woodstove.
Then, she heard him
feed the fat wood
to the embers. She heard
crackling, snaps, the
whoosh of flame
catching hold, coaxed
again from docility to rage.
The clanking close
of heavy black doors.
The heat inside.
That true noise of fire:
flames beating
against the firebox
as if an animal
just aware of its cage.
And she heard him
groping back to her
through the unsure

darkness, his body again
cooling along
the journey from flame.
She listened as he reached
for the footboard, hand
over hand, and then a
pause, and
within his pause,
she heard
the fine dry crack,
she heard the break
that did not splinter,
nor tear,
but split finely,
cleanly; its finality
racing along
the long fault
and though
finally he lay down
beside her, she had
become what he could
not see—a white
bear, icy fur clinking
like chimes
in the wind, now
adrift in a bed, a floe,
broken free.

First Hours Married

Deep into our wedding
night, I sat, white full dress
hitched and wet to my waist,
and kicked my bare feet

through the warm water.
Through the black night,
the lighted pool sparkled
like an aquamarine,

a stone I had just then
known to wish for
in my ring. The round pool
lights glowered like plates

set at a family table in the future.
In the water's current, a black
champagne bottle bobbed
and around the courtyard,

each window dark, each
door shut, but for one,
at the far end, cracked
open, asking me to see

the light shining through
that glowed, asking me
to read the yellow letter *L*
impressed upon that night.

MY LOVER IS LIKE THE BRIGHT SUN

Like the sun, awash in its own rising and setting,
unmistakably radiant you are

in your yellow comes and goes,
your weathering hand turning the brass doorknob.

You slip in and out with such honeyed ease.
Your shadow leaves too, at last.

Stirring all night, I wonder about the family
you are feeding on the other side of the world.

PRAYER TO STONE

Lord God! How could we have lived there
knowing they slunk and slithered where
ever we stirred about? The day we moved
in, a corpulent black snake lolled
across the bare scratchy yard. I pointed
it out to you. "Good Omen," I insisted,
though you teased that I never came
off the rotting porch. The ancient house

crumbled beneath our feet; nevertheless,
I believed it all could be saved. I aimed
to love even the old lumpy snake. We
stayed on, fed the red-eyed woodstove. We
hammered on. We painted. In the spring,
you pried open the old attic hatch and
they fell, dropped wriggling like long rain

that splashed about your feet. A ripe nest
of newly hatched copperheads. The old farmer
down the road offered up his remedy. We
peered over the truckbed. Nine feet long.
Its slim head lolled to the side, nearly
severed by his wife's hoe. He was proud
of the dead snake—of his wife! *Hang it*

from the tree! They'll stay away! His milky
blue eye gleamed. When he drove off
through our yard, the snake lay in the grass
until we dragged it into the brush
with a pointed stick. Who wants to hang
towels and sheets next to a carcass
blowing from a tree?

We plumbed on,
even after the dog howled and
I went under to drag him out. I crawled
beneath the house on my belly. Two fang
marks—wet and red—oozed, his black leg
swelling to an overripe eggplant. And one
night, as we lay in bed, I turned, looked
to see that through a knot hole a snake rose

as if charmed, wavered, and slowly looked me
in the eye. Then, I leapt (like an angel)
and landed atop the dresser. And perched
there, still I resolved this was not enough
to make us quit. I climbed down, knowing
if we could make it through this, we could
survive it all. Then, a phone call. A serpent

winding through your father's chest. The after-
noon we left to go back home, if I'd turned
to look back, I would have seen
our newly painted house, its red tin roof
lit up, afire in the sun. I would have stayed stone
there forever, but your father would not
have withered. Mine would not have been found

dead and alone in a shack. The sky
would have remained sealed.
But, I flinched first. I did not bear it.
And then came the revelation that rose
stone by stone into a high strong pillar:
The world is a hurtful glory
to move through. *Lord. God.*

KITCHEN OF MY HEART

Come into the kitchen of my heart. See
       where things are made
yeasty, where they rise
               and warm. See lemons
in a wicker basket.

And in a vase, a single hydrangea,
       lavender and blossom-heavy.
"Kiss the Cook" entreats the apron on a peg.

But watch out. Now
        and then,
my copper-bottomed
           pans tell lies.

There are other failures, too.

Beautiful books disappoint.
       Crazed plates and un-puzzled onions
         make us bawl.
                  The ridiculous dried cherries.

Fruit flies buzz, persist, and drone
           over freckled bananas.

Those measured cups
     of sex. My oven door
     bangs
         shut, causes birthday cakes
to fall. Any doors left open,
just irritate.   Get slammed.

In that drawer, the one
with the pretty glass knob,
we both know what hides in wait.
A long blade with a gleaming
crescent curve.   A tremble.
                                   A cleaver. That utensil,
essential. After the iron skillet
is brandished

through the garlicky
thick air.

A WOMAN ONCE GAVE US A HAMPER

And it was a blond wicker thing, long gone, long
gone slack and unsure. She is long gone too—
a few months after our wedding. So odd,
isn't it? That as cancer scaled her lungs
for that short painful ride, she should
think of us, at a time when we thought
of no one else, and she did go to
the catalog, and order that hamper
for us; and long, long, many years after
it was dragged out and at the curb slumped
sadly in the morning rain, I think of her
each time I am faced with that
lone and inscrutable black sock.

New Year

When she sees the pearl in her locket has been lost
from its socket, quickly her eyes scan the carpet,
searching for the opal orb. She drops to hands
and knees, knowing she will be blamed for this,
too, the loss, the carelessness with which she fell. Outside,
her husband drags the Christmas tree, wrapped in a tarp
like a corpse. She peeks over the sill and looks down
as he shoves it into the back of the SUV. It is morning, clear
and bright. He now slaps one hand against the other,
brushes the needles from his trousers. He looks around
and smiles. No one is awake yet. No one is watching.

PROMISE

You leave. Drive away. Around
the curve, a half-mile from here,
your convertible slips under the star-lit
canopy of sycamore leaves. White bones
march alongside the creek by the road:
take their warning. Underneath it is dark,
yet lighted birds swoop as if in an aviary.

Underneath is a house where
a woman lives: you don't know
she likes to sleep with the windows
open at night to listen for your car.

You don't know because you haven't
yet spent the night with her or you don't
know because you never thought to ask.
Now the cicadas cry, cut louder. Sinister
bird song falls from the trees. It is
possible for you to drive through
and come out the other side where
the pasture waits—open for miles,
long grass soft as my hair
in your hands. It is.

BLASON

Even a non-believer like me remembers
that Jesus held a church isn't a structure,
but its people. These many years I have slept
with you, made our children with you, and still
after love, lean to rest my head on you,
and consider the mysteries of your good
and decent heart, its thump and stomp,
its clapping chorus raising to the rafters
of your chest. I reach for your hand, intertwine
our fingers, know here are the people—
all this as I slip, fall, and tumble safely
into that sky of greening sleep.

PART TWO

BLUE HERON

When she asks, I will tell my daughter
I lost my virginity in the blond grass
beside a quick-moving river
of blackened blood. I was loved, I will say,

and well cared for. My body was a purple
silk valise and I was gently unpacked
with great curiosity. Out came all those things
my soft hands had folded away. The bells

of lily of the valley, a red-leather Bible
that fit in the palm. A blue heron unfolded
its long legs and climbed out, then flew
above us; its shadow made a cross that moved

slowly back and forth over the field. There
was the yellow watchful eye of the owl too.
And then there were things to repack:
fuchsia peonies the size of cabbages

in an old woman's garden, grape
hyacinths, the return of the lilies
proud chime, faith, no regret, no
ache for re-beginning.

Nude Model

The first time her tangerine kimono slips
from her shoulders, I think she looks pretty

good for her age and I should know because
she's about my age, but the dark and limber

girls in my drawing class, suck in
their gasps, and I find them tittering

during their cigarette break on the steps outside.
They are most concerned with her breasts, their droop

and brown sag. The zig and zag of stretch marks,
the way pulled nipples glance down. But what

do I have to throw back but the yellowish
ooze of colostrum and the toothy joy

of small things that find their own snuffling
ways to the heart? Their smooth bland faces

tell me not to bother. I know this would be nothing
to them but the moth-eaten and rag when compared

to the way their boyfriend's wet mouths
slip up on them in the middle of night.

When, for critique, our drawings go up
on the wall, I see the girls have chosen

to draw the soft folds of her orange robe,
the philodendron's shiny leaves which trail

behind the pose. The high tight arch of her
foot is the only part of her body they have considered

as art. But I've returned again and again to her
breasts; with slip of charcoal in my hand, I do study

after study. Fluid ink. I give into
paint pen, conte. Wild sweep of pink pastel.

Each class I come back to her slandered
curves and color her green and blue, sometimes

rose, sometimes purple; I portray her
as turned land and falling water,

though I know even if it were
possible for these fallow girls to imagine

it, this is no garden
they would choose to enter.

Always a Bridesmaid

What she saw, double-quick, lickety-split out
her door, swung on a line in front of her, a fat
articulated caterpillar hanging from
the thinnest strand of silk, twirling

in the air before her, as if a necklace
only just begun to be beaded.
What a thing to wear, she thought,
and touched her slack neck,

a necklace of bright green caterpillars,
head to bottom, head to bottom; it was
what she imagined on her way to the church
and even later, as the ham-handed gawky

boy in a limp tuxedo held out his fingers
to her as she exited the ridiculously stretched
limo. She wished her shoes were dyed
the color of limes, the hue of exotic tree

frogs and coconut hull, a color to match
her necklace and not the puerile taffeta
and puffy sleeves. And later, lining up
for the procession, and walking forward

in step, she felt a flutter at her throat,
blurred wings (oh, of course, it would happen
as no such thing, but just this once let
the bridesmaid have her own way,

let her choose her favorite color,
let her look down to see her green
necklace turning to flowers, then flying away,
into seven different skies and many odd graces).

WEDDING RING

She said: My darling green and slick   fish of a daughter, still
sealed tight I unwrap this   to show you the only
one left behind with me,   not to give a perfect
circle the fine minister   said, said at the altar
when it was slipped upon   me did the slip upon
me and now here it is,   walked off my thin finger
forever (perhaps) and   yet somehow still at home
now in my palm, see? Look   at this, a heavenly
loop. It's a butterscotch   on the wet tongue, halo
around the sly lamppost   on a cold rain-flung street,
gin ring at the stemmed base   of a quick martini,
green olive left behind   with pimento sucked out
full ripe kiss remembered   on a cocktail napkin,
the bombast and charming   lure of a shining hoop
snake rolling dark rolling   out of a dream, just one
swinging handcuff yet left   at the bedpost, yellow
frost around the stunned eye   of the gaffed sailfish, stiff
lens of spy glass, burnished   beetle spinning, spinning
on its back, seen only   once the tree has fallen,
after lightning has struck   that delicious winking
secret delicious and,   yet untold, that winking
secret that begs to be   fished out of its deep and
narrow hole, perhaps you   are who you think you are,
or perhaps you are your   mother's daughter or perhaps
you are your father's. Know   this now, standing here in
the bright triangle of moon   light on the knotted floor:
There are some rings woman   shouldn't hand down to daughters,
should not mind misplacing,   should not stoop to un-wrench
the kitchen pipes to retrieve,   but rather, and merrily,
should allow the faucet's   full cold flush to carry
them off and into the swift   current of mean and sour rivers.

THE BOOT OF ITALY

Black ice they call it—that surface
I was steering through without realizing,
until I saw the orange Fiat coming toward
me, at a slant, the man's face scrunched
in curse; but for some reason, I was unafraid,
even while spinning the wheels away
and even when my old station wagon began
to slide, our two cars coming head-on, fish-
tailing at each other in a slithering mechanical
rumba. Perhaps it was because the moment
had its own peculiar slow grace, the whipping
snow, the blurred neon lights of the shops
we slid by, the violet darkening of evening
sky and gravity's pull toward this man
I was about to know, at least a bit.

After the grind and last walloping
whack, and I was unhurt completely
(though my heart whirred
and I would never see that old car again),
the policeman gave me a lift to work
since he, too, was headed to the other
side of town. He put me in the backseat
and it was like grabbing a cab really,
being driven through the noisy streets
of a town where I'd only just suddenly
arrived and knew no one. And the snow
continued coming down and the officer drove
through signals he ignored and against traffic
and blipped his siren even when it wasn't
necessary. Each time the cop soared and slid
around a corner, I was hefted against

the door as if I were trying to wrench
it open, get free, but then I caught
the policeman's eyes in the rearview and
he was having a great time sliding
through the streets of our town,
enjoying the first snow of the season
with a plumped heart and just then
how could I not think of the sour man
I lived with? There in the backseat I realized
I should call the wedding off!
                                    I began to imagine
then, each time I slid against the door
I was closer and closer to breaking
a little more free of him. On Market,
I began to imagine, heaving his things
out that window. I was in a rhythm,
after that, out went his how-to books,
his absurdly neat collection of running shoes,
his need to be babied, his ugly
sister. Hmm . . . *him!*

And then the officer glided
into the empty and pristine parking lot
of the restaurant where I worked
and he hopped out with a skip and a
slip, but recovered! He recovered
and rushed to open my door.
The whole downtown
was white like that southern village
in the boot of Italy, snow drifting
up into hives stuporing at the top of houses.
From the entry, the maitre d' gestured

to me *hurry! hurry!* but I was not ready
to do more work and I would

not. My footprints in the snow,
the one and only time I looked back,
were small blue fish
swimming happily, following
in the wake behind me.

FORGIVE

Short, really short, I said, but I was in fact, not thinking
of him, was looking out the wide windows, the traffic passing
in front of the shop, I was thinking of the hurry
caused by his sports, friends laid off, feuds
with dim bureaucrats, anthrax, and dirty suitcase
bombs—his father's newly diagnosed hernia—so
when she said, "That short enough?" And finally, I
looked back to my ten-year-old son, I gasped
at the swath shorn, the wide path of stubble across
the back of his head. His scalp was like a plucked
ridiculous bird, a prisoner-of-war, vulnerable.
His was the punishment of the bog people.
His crime? To have a mother whose head could be turned
from him so easily.

      But then, what was there left to do,
but go on with it. I smiled into the mirror, shrugged
as if to say oh well. It'll grow back. Though I realized,
then, I'd missed something more important—
his just becoming aware of what it is
to be seen in the world on another's terms.
And in that broad mirror, that magnifying glass, his eyes
trapped mine—were the unforgiving and blistering sun,
and I began to feel the smoke rise inside me,
the smoldering ruin that my carelessness cost,
and his furious attempt to turn this poem to cinders.

THE EMPTY LOT

For years, foolishly, the gray shell
of basement stood unfinished, filled
and drained with the weather, with
snakes and small azure lizards
and slime, but never minding,
we lowered ourselves into all of it, expertly,
covertly, ignoring our parents' threats

to keep away from that hole. But down
we anyway went into its open grave,
its gray muck trying to suck
us under. It was worth lying,
disobeying more than one commandment
to know I was somewhere I couldn't be
seen, but could see what appeared
to be everything, *sky, sky,*
sky! I know why prisons have roofs!

Even when the perfect crosses
of jet trails hung overhead to remind,
I hunkered down, dug in the mud
with my hands, flipped over
flat rocks to witness the little paths
tunneled beneath. Squatting
there, I remained hard-jawed, defiant.

GREEN BIKE

Upon waking, I realized it was the first present
he'd bought me on his own. When I turned past
the platoon of lawn mowers, the broad bronze
and avocado washers, I knew immediately
what we'd come after. There beyond the sexy curves
of the European racers, and the wide tires
of the all-terrain—I stopped, knowing
he was headed toward sweet lime
green and daisies, the wicker basket and pink.
He leaned over the handlebars, pushed it back and
forth, then with satisfaction, nodded to me
Yes! Yes! This is it! "What do you think! *Nice*, huh!"

"Nice," my mother later repeated, spooning gray peas
onto my plate, "Wasn't it nice of your father?"
Even then I knew what I was supposed to be.
Even then I was afraid of hurting him;
it would be like treating a stranger rudely.
Nice. Be nice. That word, frozen at its center.

Even after he's dead all these years, I still want
to be nice. But, what was rising in me
then was not. Huddled upstairs, I heard
his car pull into the drive, after traveling
all week, the garage door opened easily
on its pulleys, rocking slightly like a surprise
just coming into the mouth—and there inside,
that black and rotten tooth. That black matte
secret of a bike sprayed with a wheezing can
of paint, chopped down, forked out,
streamer-less, and stripped of all lime green.

In his absence, I had pedaled all week
through bare fields, pumping furiously,
dared to do it, I gained speed, and *up*, *up*
the ramp, then I lifted high into the air,
reaching for him in my own way,
reaching as I do in all dreams of him now.

NEW DOG, OLD DOG

It's a lesson he needs
to learn, I comfort myself
when I hear my son rocking
his ruined heart to sleep
after the death of our old dog,
cancer found after finally we took serious
its refusing to eat.

It's a thing to be shown
can be lived through;
this first unleashing of sorrow
may even save my son some day.
But there's more for me to learn
too, I have to admit, seduced by
this new dog we've brought in

to keep the other old girl company,
and soften her own inevitable ending.
It's easier to pretend death is missing
from our house, as I make this
young tail-thumping one
sit and beg for the chicken left
over from dinner. I watch him gobble down,

crazy clear-eyed dog, but am listening for
the limping clatter of the other,
who may be old, but has lived here
long enough to know what's what.

Any minute she may catch on, push her old
arthritic bones up and come limping around
the corner into the kitchen to catch me
in my new and florescent infidelity;

I'm guilty, but I don't care
enough to stop. I'm like the old man
who believes I can be saved
by taking a young wife.

AUBADE

There, in a cheap motel, just off
the highway (why pay more for
six hours of sleep?), it is the quiet
gurgle that causes me to leap from bed—
that stirring, full of an urgency
only one who loves
can hear, the way a baby wakes
a mother by simply moving
differently in the night.

Blood pours from his nose.
The sink fills with it. It runs
Dracula-like from his mouth.
The white vanity top turns red.
The beautiful words leave:

He is hemorrhaging in a Super 8,
outside Calhoun, Georgia. Looking up,
in the mirror his eyes raise. He acknowledges
what we both already know: Our mistake is
grave, traveling too soon after his surgery.

After the bleeding mercifully stops, it's that
look of his that keeps falling through me,
repeating and repeating *I am leaving you.*

Onto the highway, heading toward rocking water
and flipping palms, I remember taking towels
down to the motel office, apologizing to
the manager as I handed over
the red sopping linen: "It just looks
like someone has been murdered."

Not someone, I realize now, accelerating, but
some *thing*. And now some thing else
has been born, and has begun driving
slowly, following behind.

SMALL TOWN JURY

For three days we'd been held
in that small stark room,

listening to the prosecuting attorney
drone on. *Domestic violence. Bail jumper.*

Drunk and driving six times.
All the things I could be doing

at home! I thought, until I caught glimpse
of something familiar in the crime

scene photo passed from hand
to hand. I'd recognized

a corner of fence and looked
and looked more closely, and

saw the Mother's Day Lily
there, perfectly pregnant and

about to bloom. *My fence!*
My lily! My son's red ball set

in the grass like an egg. And
in the foreground, in the car's trunk,

what the detective said were all
the makings for a drug lab. *Meth,*

the detective explained. *Something wrong?*
he asked, noting my sudden interest.

No. I quickly passed
the snapshot on. But

my neighbor, *poor, poor stupid
boy* we'd thought each time

we'd rushed to help
when the clumsy thing

set his house afire. Three times
in the middle of the night

I had waited in the door
for my husband to return.

He'd come back, shaking
his head. We both watched

the fire trucks pulsing
like fair rides at night,

and as they pulled away,
how we'd shook our heads,

feeling sorry for the kid,
stupid kid, couldn't fry baloney

for a sandwich without catching
the house on fire. *Stupid. Stupid.*

FIELD TRIP TO THE NEIGHBORHOOD FIREHOUSE

We file out back where a sleepy firefighter
yawns and strikes a match. He wants to impress
upon the children how quickly something can go
wrong. The old mattress alights in a violent whoosh,
and both chaperones and children gasp and stutter backward,
but not Charlotte, one of my charges, whose mother,
she's whispered, has just moved out of her house.

When the pin-striped ticking bursts open, flames lick
and leap taller than her teachers. Charlotte pulls
me away from the heat. Face brave, she shows me
the little campfires in her eyes that rear and blaze.

ECHO LAKE

When it rains and thunders
on the big mossy lake,
women toss in their beds,
not yet knowing they are
alone there, that their husbands
have risen into the black hot
of early morning and have pushed
their boats away from the rickety docks.
Quietly, quietly (*hush!*), the men row
across dark water, watch lightning's
narrow cracking in the dark bone
of sky, laugh and shake their heads
at the mention of return. Searchers will find
them later, sitting but still in the boat,
after the women have been roused
by the memory of thunder, after
they have measured out the coffee
and begun to listen to the hearts
straining to beat inside percolators
on the stoves, after they have gone
to the cabin windows, and gone back
to cabin windows to look out
at the brightening skies.

DEER

Asleep for an hour or more, I had not heard his key
        enter the lock, nor the door creak open,
                but his voice wakened me and I lay listening.

It was formal, but fretful, into the telephone.
        On the way home, a mile away, he'd come round
                a corner, a hard sharp curve, and almost run over

a deer, still alive, still living in the heart of the road.
        As my husband essed to a stop, the animal's head raised,
                eyes lit by the headlights of the truck.

Its muzzle quivered when he approached it and knelt,
        his shoes entering the soft current of blood.
                its hindquarters crushed, it lay caught

there in the mercy of oncoming traffic, which at that time
        of night could be scant, but also precarious.
                "I have no way to dispatch it,"

my husband apologized into the phone. He asked our sheriff,
        "Can you send someone out? It's suffering."
                When he came into our bedroom to find me

awake and as we lay under the gray moonlight
        covering our bed, he described what he had seen.
                Its calm. It must have been in shock,

seemed to be waiting for him to help, though
        the only thing left to do, he couldn't have done,
                for we had never owned a gun. We lay there,

wheeling our conversation slowly to other things—
        the children's schedules, what time we'd be getting home
                from work, while I tried to abandon the image

of the deer. We talked on softly and then heard, off
        in the dark distance—a shot. The next morning,
                as I drove by, taking the children to school,

I noticed the stain in the road; and every time I drove
        into the curve, I began to see the deer,
                the animal I'd never seen at all. As I approached,

it turned its head toward me: I looked into its eyes. It looked
        into mine. And somehow, I remembered—
                I was sixteen—had just begun driving

and was with a car filled with other girls. We roamed
        the back rural roads of our county
                heady as huntsmen (though the truth was

we were afraid of what we were stalking and trembled
        when we thought of them). And once, on a foggy night,
                we drove out of a curve and found a figure

looming ahead in the road. We slowed, coasting
        toward it, headlights useless too far into the fog,
                but still it was a shape, erect, a small man,

I thought. No, a child! All voices finally quieted in the car
        as we coasted toward it; we were frightened!
                We dreaded that we were going to—at last—

see something! And then, the car rolled to a stop
        in front of a colossally feathered owl.
                Gray feathered! Stormy white-brinked wings.

Tall as we had been when we began school!
        In the road, like a sentinel it blocked our way home
                to our parents who were at the windows,

looking down the long farm roads for us. It blocked
        our way to the party in the field, where bonfires
                would keep us safe if we stood near,

safe from the things that invited us to the edge of the woods.
        The owl would not move, would not move, but
                only blinked its amber eyes. It gulped

and a ripple moved through its body. A girl whispered
        from the back seat. *Honk at it!* But I couldn't.
                Wouldn't for some reason. I could open the door

and I quietly shooed it. Nothing. My best friend, the girl
        who would not live at home, who went
                into the woods every chance she could, stood

warrior pose in the road. "Move along!" she commanded, arm
        lifting to levitate, but even she scrambled back into the car
                when the willows began to twitch,

the forest reaching out for us. The wind raised
        and we all wanted to go home and a girl in the backseat
                began to weep, but she laughed, too, knowing

it was silly. And it was. It was only an owl.
How many times had we lain in bed at night
and heard them ask us our names?

It was, only then, when we all began to think of ourselves
as ourselves that the owl finally grew tired of us,
though to punctuate that it would only move

slowly and of its own accord, it looked left, and then
right and then extended its long long wings
and raised slowly into the sky, flying directly over

my head. I looked into its soft belly, bits of grass yet caught
in its talons, curved and black-tipped and yellow.
I can still hear the whoosh, whoosh of its wings

gathering wind, and then flying off over my head and
then it was gone into the night.
It was magnificent.

Caught and held in my mind is the place between
earth and heaven. And how have I ended up
here, wandering far from that night

my husband rushed home to call the sheriff, leaving inside me
the image of the deer,
half crushed, lying suffering

in their road? *Deer. Owl. Flight.* I am offered
yet again the lesson: How the yellow hand of the glorious
opens its own window for return.

PART THREE

Why I Mother You the Way I Do

That afternoon, I have to admit, there were no thoughts
of you. I was in high school, making my way past
the buses to a waiting car—a boy who would not be
your father—when the line of traffic stopped. The girls,
classmates, sisters, had darted between buses
and into the highway, trying to cross the field to their home.
They both lay twisted in the road. My science teacher,
Mr. Desaro, took off his suit coat and laid it over Susan's
face. He was crying because he only had one coat.

By the time they let us pass, Eve had been covered with a white
sheet. The ambulances had come. Red lights flashed, but
their mother was still pushing her silver cart
through the grocery. The sheriff was walking up behind
her. As she reached for a gallon of milk, he moved
to touch her arm.

DARK POND WITH IRIS

The bold bullfrog's luminous eyes
seemed dazed, I thought, then no,

cartoonishly amazed, then finally, I saw
them in their fixed stubbornness,

his cheeks puffed out in defiant stead.
The small garter snake had caught him

from behind, and the snake's undulating
muscle mercilessly and deliberately worked

its mouth up and over the frog's back
in agonizing millimeters. An appalling thing

to see at the edge of our goldfish pond!
My daughter knelt there too, watching

awhile, but soon ran back to her tire swing
after the frog took no notice of us,

his cheeks still full of air and quiet
concentrated fight. It was only later,

when I came back to see him almost
swallowed down, his small green cone

of face not crowning, but disappearing,
that I realized this is so contrary to the way

I must have come into the world, passively
being worked down the dark birth canal,

sliding out with eyes stuck closed,
not even minutely aware of the beginning

of this miracle: that one day I'll likely
fight this hard to stay in a world

I have exerted no will
or muscle to enter.

My Thirteen-Year-Old Son,
the Fisherman, Throws One Back

At the end of the buckled pier,
my son flung far out his line which
seemed imagined until lit by the sun.
From time to time, I looked up

from reading when commotion filled
the frail pier. His reeling frame arched,
rod bending, releasing its punishing
whine. Five full days on the coast

and he hadn't caught anything worth
keeping. *How can you love it so much?*
I'd asked, watching him once again straighten
and classify the plastic wriggling tackle.

But I'd been told before and shouldn't have
had to wonder. It's the *possibility*
he loves, the imagined on the end of
the line, those few moments when the hooked *could*

be halibut or shark, though soon what surfaces
is a channel cat or worse, a flat rubbery ray,
slit mouth widening its ugly gasp. Later, on the beach,
nearly naked girls romped nearby, tried hard

to catch his eye. Watching them throw back
their long dark hair, I wondered how many
of them were about to jump his line? How many
swam just there, beneath the surface, promising

to be the long-dreamed-after silver bullet
of hooked tarpon? At the water's edge,
that night I discovered the ray, moonlit,
gashed, floating weakly in the black surf—

only then would I recall how my son
had glanced back at the girls, lifting
his head in an aggressive nod, as I'd seen
other boys do when they imagined themselves

grown men. I had to admit too, how, that morning,
like an assassin, he'd cut the line, then casually kicked
the wounded creature across the pier, until it fell back
into the ruffling, heart-colored upset of the sea.

BLUE CANOE

Today, God was the red-chinned buzzard that caught
the boys' attention and moved their eyes to the side
of the barn where the sun illuminated the blue canoe

and God was the idea that became a tug on the sleeve
of the t-shirt and the words "come on," and God
was the path through the field and the rain that began

to fall as the boys pulled the canoe through, parting
the tall gold grass, leaving the appalling trail behind
them and God made the rain come down harder

around them, pocking Floyd's Fork into swelling
and God was the laughter and loud language
and gleeful paddling through the current

that went wilder, but also the tree that snatched
the canoe and flipped it, trapping the boys underneath
and God was the air that rested inside the hull and

the 911 call to the sheriff made by the passerby
and the voice of the sheriff as he radioed
and God was in the ring of the phone call

that one father picked up and God was the hand
of the other steering through rush-hour
traffic, and in the tall shadows of men

who waited on the bank and God was there too,
giving hope, until the canoe could be recovered,
uncovering the last breaths, and then he was not.

BACK YARD

Beneath the flowers, corpulent beetle
grubs, the color of old teeth, lay dormant
and tightly muscled. Over, though, the blue moth
comes to the cup of the lily, and moves like a flickering
electric light, like a weak star exposing the possibility
of night when she might slip undetected
from their bed, and be left alone to do as she truly wishes,
to crawl through the back yard to search in moonlight
and without judgment for the footsteps all others
want forgotten. Slowly downhill, she would move
and methodically, through the sour turn
of composting leaf and toward the edge of woods
where she could sleep in the dead boy's fort
which stands empty, too, and falling back
into the earth's cold embrace.

FORTUNE

Ted was a person who liked to go back through things,
        meticulously, and with extended patience;
sorting and unfolding bits of paper and receipts comforted him,

gave him a sense of order. Imagine then, his loss,
        after the death of his son, when Ted's wallet came up
missing—would never be found, though he could not know

that then. While bereaved at his diminishment, slowly,
        Ted did begin again to make out the moving,
the lemon finch hovering at the feeder, his wife

in the lily garden, the blue and red globes of hot air balloons
        that traveled over the fields of his home. Often
they floated so near, Ted could hear their fires,

see them shoot up, and the dark figures waved to him.
        Ted could never, though, shake his grief
at his inability to open his old familiar wallet, and realized one morning

something he had missed dearly: that crazy slip of fortune his son
        thought so funny: "There are happy times for you
in store." Which store? Benny had kidded. The grocery

or the quickie mart? The store where they picked up auto parts?
        And how Ted wished most for a bit of note left after
an argument, when they both sat silently at the kitchen table,

and his son slyly pushed a folded message through the loop
        of the handle of Ted's coffee cup. "Please
Dad," Benny had written, "Just please let it go."

REMARRIAGE

My body
has been
re-sealed
like a red
envelope;
I've a long
letter inside.
Steam me
open. Read.

SEED

In first grade, you met Squanto,
nearly naked and
on his haunches, showing
those thick-headed pilgrims
how one must plant fish
to grow maize. And in autumn
you dove into the lobotomized
pumpkin, into the gooey pulp
and seeds, raising a clump
like a slimy chandelier
from the Titanic. And now
in late summer, daughter,
you smile, holding a ripe watermelon,
cut in half, exposing the black
seed within its bright red heart.
Your melon. How proud you are
to think you grew this delicious
thing all on your own.

FAMILY RECIPE

The blue eye flares.
A black pot, lid chattering.
Grandmother's sullen ghost
slowly climbs the foggy stairs.

Break hard spaghetti
in two. Crack it like bone—
stir the broth to soothe.
What feeds must be fed.

Around and around moves
the wooden spoon, softening
bone, softening the bone.

Hilltop Farm

The fields of the farm next door are
 all wrong. In the winter they are brittle

and icy with your loss; in the spring,
the rivulets from hard rain try to wash

the old blood in the path left when you struggled
up the hill. The expressway below, where you were

dumped and rolled into a ravine and left for dead,
becomes a place to stop, not to go, go on, and

the cows in the field, once proud Black Angus seem
to understand that they, too, are on their way

to market. They learned it that night, when under
the hard black sky, you crawled by, pulling yourself

up one handful of grass after another and under
the fence and into their fields where with large eyes—

circling in their sockets, circling like planets loosening
from gravity, the cows stamped nervously. Their breath

streamed over the fields like white poison gas,
so that now in summer what grows cannot nourish—

and the swans are not swans anymore—they were
not bought as hatchlings by the farmer to amuse

his young wife, bored and vain as Emma Bovary—
no, the swans are now what they were that time,

fierce and disquieting. You were, for part of that night
anyway, their golden egg. When you came to

the edge of the pond to drink, to revive, they floated
in to become your feathered altar. All night you had

struggled up the hill and toward the edge of
the gravel drive, where you thought you might

find a way, your stiletto broken from its lamé
sandal, your shorts soaked through. The halter

knot tightening at the back of your neck. By then,
of course, he had driven away. The arrogance of it,

his turning on the blinker to ease back into traffic,
to drive across town to his small brick house,

to boil water in a saucepan for instant coffee, to keep
an eye on the early morning news. The field is not

the field; nor can it ever be again. Though as it
changed, I slept on in a white house next door

which used to be a church. Perhaps you knew that?
Perhaps you remembered coming here with

your ardent aunties, who swayed and swooned
when the preacher led the hymns with his big

baritone voice. Perhaps, that's where you thought
the gravel road led. But this is not a church

anymore; and I did not wake. I did not
know about wakening.

OPENING

What I remember is that I had watched you leave
        the bed, and it was late spring and the window
    was open because I had asked you to raise it,
           and you had not argued, but done it. I heard
   water running and the white sheer curtain
blew into the room like a bride's veil caught
           in a sudden whip of wind
    as she hurried out of the church, alone.

The traffic below passed by. Remarkably orderly schoolchildren were passing by
    in the street, and the sky was stolid, as serious and blue
          as the eye of an old preacher sitting at the side
of a bed. Then, for an instant, a cloud darkened the room

      as if the sky had winked at me. I knew I was leaving.
I suppose I had known it for a long while, but just then
    I was happy to have that one moment of winky blue sky to return to
when I caught my toe and stumbled back into this time
      through the many years later.

MORNING'S CHORES

Through the lilac mist, they slip along the edge
      of the old graveyard
                like spirits. The plot so full
one hundred years before
we moved next door
        that I often forget they may come.
      It's mid-spring, warming, but
      they're dressed for winter: flannel shirts, long dark jeans, heavy ochre-colored boots.
I've just sent my children off on the school bus, and since the boy
      was found in the river, I prefer to stay, to watch, until
              the bus toddles around the curve,
      until there's nothing more to see. This morning
I've taken my coffee to the laundry room
      to begin to sort and bleach.
                 Steam rises from the washer
      as I lean into the mounded hampers
           and cast off dirty socks or undershirts
to make piles of dark
and light. I lower and raise,
      and find, looking through the window that I seem to be
      echoing their movements as they shovel out the hole.
            One man is in the hole
      to his waist; the other, the one with the ponytail, stands above,
leans on a shovel. He's laughing, then slowly turns my way,
      as if he's glanced me at the window.
He seems to wave—a quick burlesque gesture—
      but then I see his flicked cigarette
      cartwheeling through the air, a Catherine Wheel,
spinning as if a small human engine fires at its center,
    throwing off an intimate light.

How to Fold

1.

It's in my laundry room where I *most*
feel The Holy Ghost. When I pull a clean
warm towel from the dryer, I stretch both arms
out—*see me*. I am a cross. Palms together,
I beseech. Remembering all the times
I have been mis-seen, I bring my
clasped hands to my chin.

2.

My mother folds her towels in her own way.
She has taken in the spirit of the Jesus and so
she flips her towels joyously through the air.
My sister has converted and now lays
her clean towel upon a table, makes creases
straight and uniform. By the good book.

3.

I used to think we would all be received;
we only need knock at the scarred door,
and the fat preacher, bald red head slick
as a waxed apple, would open it slightly.
But one must beg, palms up to enter. One must
be drained. One must declare: My towels
are folded, stacked—*clean*, they no
longer smell of my daughter's pink
flushed body. My son's dark hand prints
have been rinsed free. I can no longer sneak
a whiff of the dank sex between my husband
and me. I am a woman with clean laundry.

4.

My lint has been wiped from its screen.

5.

I wait for preacher to take my hands in his own.
He sits me in a hard chair before
the bright window and helps me see
for myself that only now
am I truly a woman come clean.

With a Shiner, My Husband Enters the Flower Shop

I should be thinking about him and how
he could have lost an eye when
the malignant scaffolding collapsed and a 2

x 4 dropped through the air on the job
site the morning of our nineteenth anniversary, but
I'm considering her, the florist

looking up from her table to see
him walking in sheepish, head-
bowed, ringing the bell as he enters.

I'm wondering how many times
she's arranged roses for the wounded,
the bruised, the stitched hungry male

who needs her help—*and fast.*
And I wonder if she imagines me,
black cast iron skillet,

cocked in hand like a baseball bat
as she pulls out the three stems
of delphinium, blue as a bruised

heart and two full hydrangea,
pink petaled and soft as boxed
lingerie. There is not, baby's breath,

I'm relieved to see, nor
the red lips of soft roses,
nor the ubiquitous and overly cheerful

mum. She knows, somehow, what
he does not—preoccupied with his day
to day—that even a good long marriage holds

small hurts that barb and fester
near the skin, so she reaches
for the balm of calm sweep

of palm leaf, that healer of the unsaid
argument of morning, the rising blood
as I watched him back out

in his truck, his having forgotten—once
again—this morning of all mornings—
to hang up the towel, curled

like a wet dog asleep on the bathroom
floor. A long marriage remembers
its youth as a roan, muscled horse, rearing,

with nostrils flared.
                              I accept this
bouquet for what I could have said
but didn't, and hold onto the thin

healing. I accept, too, finally, that often
a long marriage is a donkey schlepping
across the desert. Tender-eyed, I attempt

to once again re-love husband as self,
to heal the wounded eye as one tries
to heal self. And accept the vase

on the table which stands to remind,
each day as I change its water,
that even this good marriage

is from time to time a sorry animal, in need,
and overburdened, but grateful for the hard
day it closes sore eyes against.

BIOGRAPHICAL NOTE

Award-winning poet and teacher Kathleen Driskell serves as the Associate Program Director of Spalding University's brief-residency Master of Fine Arts in Writing Program in Louisville, Kentucky. She is the author of one previous book of poetry, *Laughing Sickness*, now in its second printing, and the editor of two anthologies of creative writing. She has been awarded an Al Smith Fellowship from the Kentucky Arts Council and grants from the Kentucky Foundation for Women. Her poems have appeared in many journals including *North American Review*, *Southern Review*, and *The Greensboro Review*. She lives with her husband and two children in an old country church built before the American Civil War. Her website address is www.kathleendriskell.org.